BIBLE
STUDIES
FOR LIFE®
SMALL GROUPS

MORE THAN ENOUGH

HOW JESUS MEETS OUR DEEPEST NEEDS

JEFF IORG

LifeWay Press® • Nashville, Tennessee

© 2015 LifeWay Press® • Reprinted 2016

ISBN 9781430043188 • Item 005756890

Dewey decimal classification: 234.2
Subject headings: JESUS CHRIST / HAPPINESS / HOPE

Eric Geiger
Vice President, LifeWay Resources

Ronnie Floyd
General Editor

Gena Rogers
Sam O'Neal
Content Editors

Michael Kelley
Director, Groups Ministry

Printed in the United States of America

Send questions/comments to: Content Editor; *Bible Studies for Life: Adults;* One LifeWay Plaza; Nashville, TN 37234-0152; or make comments on the Web at *BibleStudiesforLife.com.*

For ordering or inquiries, visit *lifeway.com;* write LifeWay Small Groups; One LifeWay Plaza; Nashville, TN 37234-0152; or call toll free 800.458.2772.

We believe that the Bible has God for its author; salvation for its end; and truth, without any mixture of error, for its matter and that all Scripture is totally true and trustworthy. To review LifeWay's doctrinal guideline, please visit *lifeway.com/doctrinalguideline.*

Scripture quotations are taken from the Holman Christian Standard Bible®, copyright 1999, 2000, 2002, 2003, 2009 by Holman Bible Publishers. Used by permission. Holman Christian Standard Bible®, Holman CSB®, and HCSB® are federally registered trademarks of Holman Bible Publishers.

Bible Studies for Life: Adults often lists websites that may be helpful to our readers. Our staff verifies each site's usefulness and appropriateness prior to publication. However, website content changes quickly, so we encourage you to approach all websites with caution. Make sure sites are still appropriate before sharing them with students, friends, and family.

contents

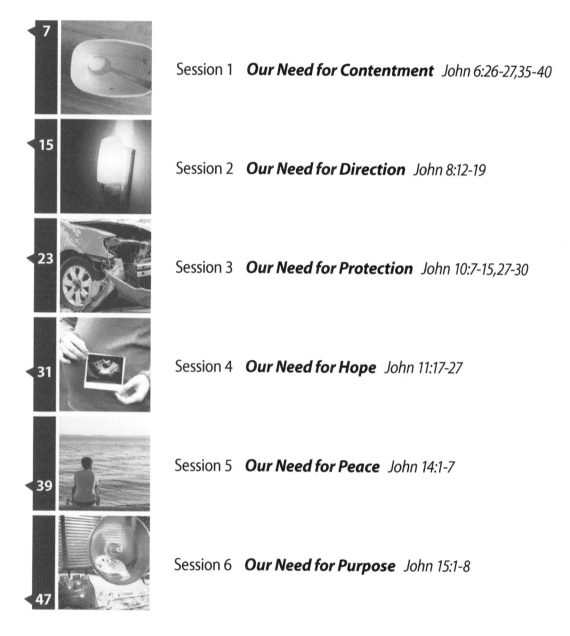

Social Media

 Connect with a community of *Bible Studies for Life* users. Post responses to questions, share teaching ideas, and link to great blog content. ***Facebook.com/BibleStudiesForLife***

 Get instant updates about new articles, giveaways, and more. **@BibleMeetsLife**

The App

Bible Studies for Life is also available as an e-book. The e-book can be opened and read with the *Bible Studies for Life App*, a free app from the iOS App Store or the Google Play Store.

Blog

At ***BibleStudiesForLife.com/blog*** you will find additional resources for your study experience, including music downloads provided by LifeWay Worship. Plus, leaders and group members alike will benefit from the blog posts written for people in every life stage—singles, parents, boomers, and senior adults—as well as media clips, connections between our study topics, current events, and much more.

Training

 For helps on how to use Bible Studies for Life, tips on how to better lead groups, or additional ideas for leading this session, visit: ***ministrygrid.com/web/biblestudiesforlife***.

ABOUT THIS STUDY

Don't deny your needs. Find whom you need.

We all long for peace, security, and fulfillment. Denying those needs is pointless. Trying to meet them in unhealthy ways is counterproductive. Languishing in frustration when they are not met is unnecessary.

God has a better plan:

▶ "I am the bread of life" (John 6:35).

▶ "I am the light of the world" (John 8:12).

▶ "I am the door" (John 10:7,9).

▶ "I am the good shepherd" (John 10:11).

▶ "I am the resurrection and the life" (John 11:25).

▶ "I am the way, the truth, and the life" (John 14:6).

▶ "I am the true vine" (John 15:1).

Are you tired of the treadmill of human effort, running on the personal fulfillment track to nowhere? Are you burned out by people—tired of being let down again and again? Are you ready to give up searching for significance at the mall or on the car lot?

For everything you need, Jesus said, "I am." And that's more than enough.

ABOUT THE AUTHOR

Jeff Iorg

Jeff Iorg is the president of Gateway Seminary in California. Jeff is a seasoned ministry leader who writes about real-life issues, not just academic theories. He is the editor of the book *Ministry in the New Marriage Culture* (B&H Publishing, 2015). Jeff is married to Ann, and they have three adult children and one awesome grandson. Learn more and find leadership insights at *jeffiorg.com*.

OUR NEED FOR CONTENTMENT

When have you recently had too much of a good thing?

QUESTION #1

#BSFLenough

Jesus is the Bread of life who gives us true satisfaction.

THE BIBLE MEETS LIFE

People today want more:

▶ The average home has 189 TV channels.

▶ We can choose from over 50 brands of toothpaste; most of those brands offer multiple choices.

▶ The seven-ounce soft drink size of 1955 has been replaced with 42-ounce cups—and larger.

So many people in our society are convinced that more is always better, bigger is always best, and getting our way always equals prosperity and happiness. It's easy to believe that if we race to the top, gain all the privileges, or have the most money—we will finally be satisfied.

Thankfully, Jesus taught a better way.

WHAT DOES THE BIBLE SAY?

John 6:26-27,35-40

26 Jesus answered, "I assure you: You are looking for Me, not because you saw the signs, but because you ate the loaves and were filled.

27 Don't work for the food that perishes but for the food that lasts for eternal life, which the Son of Man will give you, because God the Father has set His seal of approval on Him."

35 "I am the bread of life," Jesus told them. "No one who comes to Me will ever be hungry, and no one who believes in Me will ever be thirsty again.

36 But as I told you, you've seen Me, and yet you do not believe.

37 Everyone the Father gives Me will come to Me, and the one who comes to Me I will never cast out.

38 For I have come down from heaven, not to do My will, but the will of Him who sent Me.

39 This is the will of Him who sent Me: that I should lose none of those He has given Me but should raise them up on the last day.

40 For this is the will of My Father: that everyone who sees the Son and believes in Him may have eternal life, and I will raise him up on the last day."

Bread of life (v. 35)—
An allusion by Jesus to manna, the white substance that tasted like wafers made with honey and was miraculously provided by God for the Israelites wandering in the desert. The psalmist called this substance "bread from heaven" (see Ex. 16:31; Ps. 78:24).

The last day (v. 40)—
A phrase embodying Jewish thought about a final judgment by God featuring the resurrection of the dead that ends history and establishes ultimate justice.

> **Why do people seek satisfaction in things that don't last?**

QUESTION **#2**

John 6:26-27

In 1928, Herbert Hoover ran for president with this campaign promise: "A chicken in every pot and a car in every garage." He was elected. Voters were drawn to the candidate who promised prosperity.

Jesus never promised prosperity, but He did something for the people that led them to think prosperity was just around the corner. Earlier in John 6, Jesus multiplied five barley loaves and two fish into enough food to feed 5,000 men—with enough leftovers to fill 12 baskets (see vv. 12-13). This was an impressive miracle that convinced people Jesus was a prophet from God who should be their king.

There's a problem with the kind of prosperity the people expected from Jesus: it doesn't last. Sure, the miracle provided a great meal for one day, but the people were hungry again the next day.

In verses 26-27 Jesus confronted their misplaced priorities. The miracle of the loaves and fishes was supposed to draw people to God, not motivate them to trail after Jesus in search of a perpetual buffet. The people were pursuing "food that perishes," but Jesus had come to offer "food that lasts," meaning eternal life, as a gift from God through the "Son of Man"—Jesus Himself.

People today often struggle with the same misplaced priorities. When we try to satisfy our deepest needs with bigger TVs, sportier cars, or fancier clothes, we waste our time and only become more frustrated. We think such material things will give us the security and significance that only comes through a relationship with Jesus.

We need to get off the "get more" treadmill and enjoy the eternal satisfaction only Jesus provides.

John 6:35

The crowd had already seen extraordinary things, but apparently that wasn't enough. They asked Jesus what sign He planned to offer so they might believe in Him. They mentioned God's earlier provision of manna for their forefathers, as if to say Jesus' recent culinary miracle was not all that special. They wanted Jesus to do a *real* miracle to establish His credibility.

We often exhibit the same self-centeredness. We ask God to prove Himself by meeting our needs or by intervening in our lives. We ignore all God has *already* accomplished—both through the work of Jesus and in our lives over the years—when we require God to act "in the moment" before we affirm faith in Him.

Jesus declared that God had given them "the real bread from heaven" and further clarified, "the bread of God is the One who comes down from heaven and gives life to the world" (vv. 32-33).

In response, the people cried out, "Sir, give us this bread always!" (v. 34). They were still thinking about themselves, expressing their desire for perpetual meal service and not yet recognizing the spiritual significance of Jesus' words.

Jesus then made His most direct statement: "I am the bread of life." He also added thirst to the metaphor. By coupling hunger and thirst, combined with the previous food miracle that had started the entire sequence, Jesus underscored His ultimate goal even more strongly. Jesus promised, "No one who comes to me will ever be hungry, and no one who believes in Me will ever be thirsty again" (v. 35).

Jesus appealed to His hearers to rise above focusing on themselves and their temporal desires for immediate gratification. He promised eternal satisfaction to every person who believes in Him—an infinitely more significant gift than food and drink.

> **When have you experienced spiritual hunger or thirst?**
>
> QUESTION **#3**

> **What does this "I am" statement teach us about Jesus' nature and character?**
>
> QUESTION **#4**

John 6:36-40

After rebuking His followers' selfishness, Jesus sought to teach them the truth by highlighting two key elements of God's work in accomplishing salvation.

First, our salvation is based on God's initiative: "Everyone the Father gives Me will come to Me" (v. 37). While it is essential for people to repent (see Acts 2:38) and place their faith in Christ to experience salvation (see Eph. 2:8-9), God always takes the first step in the salvation process. He sent Jesus as our Savior, empowered His resurrection, and assured His ascension. God's plan for salvation has been set in place since before He created the world (see Eph. 1:4-5).

Still, acknowledging God's initiative doesn't diminish our need to respond. God prompts, convicts, and draws people to Himself. Yet repentance and faith are also biblical essentials for salvation. God invites people into a relationship with Him, and that relationship is sealed through our repentance and faith.

Second, Jesus taught that our relationship with God is permanent:

▶ "The one who comes to me I will never cast out" (v. 37).

▶ "This is the will of Him who sent Me: that I should lose none of those He has given Me but should raise them up on the last day" (v. 39).

How would you describe your experiences with the "bread of life"?

QUESTION **#5**

Remember that the permanence we enjoy in our relationship with God is guaranteed by His power, not our efforts. God draws people into salvation and then sustains their eternal relationship with Him.

Nothing at all can threaten your relationship with Jesus (see Rom. 8:38-39). We can finally find true contentment when we base our lifestyle choices on this profound truth. We are no longer hungry, thirsty people striving to satisfy eternal cravings with earthly possessions, achievements, or accomplishments. We are secure in God through our connection to Jesus Christ.

MEETING NEEDS

Below is a list of some deeper needs that all people experience. Choose two items on that list and record how our culture typically encourages us to meet those needs.

Purpose

Wellness

Love

Security

Hope

How has Christ met one of these needs in your life?

LIVE IT OUT

How will you respond to the Bread of life this week? Consider the following options for seeking out even greater contentment:

▶ **Give it up.** Identify something temporary you have been pursuing as a means of security—a possession, an achievement, an accomplishment, and so on. Stop your pursuit. Repent and ask God to grant you true contentment in Jesus.

▶ **Give thanks.** Commit to expressing gratitude this week when others serve or bless you. Thankfulness is a great way to avoid self-centeredness and promote satisfaction.

▶ **Give it away.** Volunteer with a ministry that serves others in need. While doing so, share the gospel with someone by using this Scripture passage to help him or her understand true satisfaction comes from Jesus Christ.

As a follower of Christ, you have access to more than you could ever hope for. Your security as a believer is eternal. You received it on the day you were saved, not on the day you die. Everything you need, and so much more, can be found in Jesus.

My *thoughts*

OUR NEED FOR DIRECTION

When do you remember feeling afraid of the dark?

QUESTION #1

#BSFLenough

Jesus is the Light who reveals the way we should go.

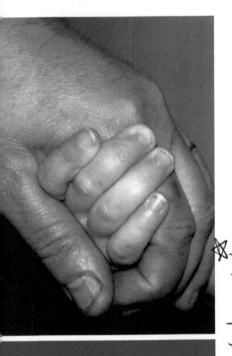

THE BIBLE MEETS LIFE

Late one Saturday night, my five-year-old son accompanied me on a quick trip to our church. It was pitch black outside as well as inside the building. The light switches were across the foyer from the entry. As we shuffled along in the dark, moving toward the switches, someone touched my hand. I screamed! My son squeezed my hand harder and said, "Don't worry, Daddy, it's me."

What a relief!

When you are surrounded by darkness, it's good to know someone is with you. It's even better to have someone turn on the lights.

As we'll see in John 8, Jesus is always with us, no matter how dark life may seem. And He does more than turn on the light. Jesus Himself *is* the Light of the world.

Camille

WHAT DOES THE BIBLE SAY?

John 8:12-19

12 Then Jesus spoke to them again: "I am the light of the world. Anyone who follows Me will never walk in the darkness but will have the light of life."

13 So the Pharisees said to Him, "You are testifying about Yourself. Your testimony is not valid."

14 "Even if I testify about Myself," Jesus replied, "My testimony is valid, because I know where I came from and where I'm going. But you don't know where I come from or where I'm going.

15 You judge by human standards. I judge no one.

16 And if I do judge, My judgment is true, because I am not alone, but I and the Father who sent Me judge together.

17 Even in your law it is written that the witness of two men is valid.

18 I am the One who testifies about Myself, and the Father who sent Me testifies about Me."

19 Then they asked Him, "Where is Your Father?" "You know neither Me nor My Father," Jesus answered. "If you knew Me, you would also know My Father."

Light of the world (v. 12)— Jesus illumines the path we are called to follow.

Darkness (v. 12)—The antithesis to light. Here, "darkness" is used as the metaphorical equivalent in religious language to evil, immorality, and other spiritual forces aligned against God.

Testimony (vv. 13-14)— A courtroom term referring to statements about which a person would swear in a court of law; in this case, it meant speaking truth about what one has witnessed about God.

light = salvation + direction

READ:
★★ Joshua ch 1
★ EXODUS
★ Psalm 25 & 27 ch.

John 8:12

Jesus had been teaching in the temple complex during the Festival of Tabernacles (see John 7:2,14). The morning after the last day of the festival, Jesus went again to the temple and began to teach. As He taught, the religious leaders brought to Him a woman who had been caught in adultery (see 8:2-11). They did so "at dawn" (v. 2). As the sun came up, the people would have been coming out of darkened houses to experience the fresh light of a new day. This helped set the stage for Jesus' incredible pronouncement: "I am the light of the world."

Notice Jesus did not claim to *provide* light to the world. He declared Himself to *be* "the light of the world."

The concept and symbolism of light is very important in the Bible. Light is used as a symbol or reference for salvation in both Old and New Testaments (see Ps. 27:1 and 1 John 1:7, for examples). When Jesus proclaimed that He was the Light of the world, He thus announced Himself as the only Source for salvation. Jesus is the only true Savior.

The Bible also uses light to symbolize God's direction. God had led His people by a pillar of fire at night during their wilderness wanderings (see Ex. 13:21-22). Appropriately, this event had just been commemorated through the Festival of Tabernacles during the time Jesus made this temple visit.

Think about the nature of Jesus' claim in an agrarian society. During a time before electricity, when light was more difficult to create and more precious to maintain, Jesus declared Himself to be light. Jesus identified Himself as a primary Source for a fundamental need among humanity.

Jesus also followed His assertion with a promise: "Anyone who follows Me will never walk in the darkness but will have the light of life" (v. 12). Jesus promised we would never be in darkness.

> **Where do you see evidence of darkness in today's world?**
>
> QUESTION **#2**

> **What does this "I am" statement teach us about Jesus' nature and character?**
>
> QUESTION **#3**

It's easy for people to become enamored with what appear to be other sources of light—worldly wisdom, media information, popular philosophies, and so on. All of these sparkle and shine to get our attention, but ultimately they lead down dark trails of frustration and desperation. Trust Jesus as the Light: your Savior and Guide.

YOUR TESTIMONY

Imagine you are called as a witness to testify about who Jesus is based on your personal experiences with Him. How would you respond? Use the space below to record your answer in a way comfortable for you—tell a story, make a list, sketch a picture, and so on.

What prevents you from sharing your experiences with Jesus more freely?

John 8:13-15

The Pharisees reacted negatively to Jesus' assertion that He was the Light of the world. Their objection was based on the law: "You are testifying about Yourself, Your testimony is not valid" (v. 13). This, however, was not the first time Jesus had heard this accusation, and He previously cited four witnesses in His defense—John the Baptist, His works, His Father, and Scripture (see John 5:31-39).

Jesus didn't disagree that valid testimony requires corroboration (see Deut. 17:6; 19:15). Therefore, He produced other witnesses to back up His declaration. The problem was the Pharisees' determination to ignore any information that contradicted their foregone conclusion that Jesus was a fraud. They weren't about to be confused by the facts.

Many religious people today have made up their minds about what constitutes spiritual "truth"—even when it contradicts the clear teaching of Scripture. Unbelievers make the same mistake by trusting in their reason, man-made philosophies, or humanistic education rather than in God's Word. No matter how unreasonable their positions may be, both groups hold fast to what they believe rather than submit to Jesus and biblical truth.

Jesus knew the truth, and He knew His testimony was valid. "My testimony is valid, because I know where I came from and where I'm going" (v. 14). He appealed to His origin and His destination as proof of His Deity. He had come from His Father and would soon return.

The Pharisees' problem was their humanistic worldview. Jesus said, "You judge by human standards" (v. 15). They started with themselves and incorporated God into their lives wherever they could. Jesus calls us to start with God as our Father and adjust our lives accordingly. He must be at the center of our lives, with everything else ordered around Him.

> **What are some reasons people give today for rejecting God's Word as truth?**
>
> QUESTION **#4**

What decisions must we make in order
to follow Jesus' judgments and directions?

QUESTION #5

John 8:16-19

Jesus came to extend salvation, not condemnation, to all people (see 3:17). He came as light to overcome darkness, not just as a judge to condemn darkness. He came as an exclusive Savior, and all people will be judged based on their choices about Him.

Continuing His testimony, Jesus used an argument based on the law—the Pharisees' ultimate source of authority: "Even in your law it is written that the witness of two men is valid" (v. 17). This was based on Old Testament passages which required at least two credible witnesses to determine guilt in a legal proceeding (see Deut. 17:6-7; 19:15). Jesus declared His claims to be true because they were based on the testimony of two witnesses—Himself and His Father. These two witnesses are the pinnacle of anyone who might be called in any judicial proceeding.

Jesus concluded this exchange with His most pointed rebuke: "You know neither Me nor my Father" (v. 19). Imagine how stunning those words must have sounded to the arrogant Pharisees who paraded themselves as public models of religious devotion. They claimed to know God; in fact, they claimed to know more about God than anyone else. Yet Jesus pronounced them to be illegitimate usurpers with no genuine relationship with the Father.

We must not make this same mistake. Jesus is the Light of the world, and God the Father is His corroborating witness. Therefore, live your life under His authority in submission to His instructions.

LIVE IT OUT

Since Jesus is the Light of the world, how will that truth influence your actions and attitudes this week? Consider taking one of the following steps in response:

▶ **Identify.** Seek out an area of your life in which you are following sources of light other than Christ. Take action to move away from those sources and follow Christ.

▶ **Submit.** Begin each day this week by verbally submitting yourself to God. Proclaim your desire to walk only in the direction revealed by the light of Christ, and continually pray for guidance throughout the day.

▶ **Study.** Read a book on Christian worldview such as *Mere Christianity* by C. S. Lewis. If possible, study this book with someone else and discuss what it teaches about following the light and direction of Jesus.

There will be times when you find yourself in darkness—our world is filled with it, after all. But you never have to be alone in that darkness. When you follow Jesus, you will always be able to find the Light.

My _thoughts_

OUR NEED FOR PROTECTION

When have you felt protected during a strange or scary situation?

QUESTION **#1**

#BSFLenough

Jesus is the only One who offers us ultimate protection.

THE BIBLE MEETS LIFE

Several years ago, while traveling in a major city, our family was using the subway on an especially crowded day. When the train arrived at our station, my wife and I surged ahead with the crowd, moving two of our children forward. We each thought the other was holding our youngest son's hand, but as the train began moving, we saw him standing in the boarding area. Alone.

We panicked. We jumped off the train at the next stop and grabbed the first train headed back in the other direction. We prayed the whole way, trying to hold back the tears, fearful of what might happen to a little boy left all alone. We arrived to find our son still standing there on the platform, wide-eyed and wondering where we had gone. In the end, all was well.

We all know the feeling of vulnerability is disconcerting, to say the least. Jesus knows life can be overwhelming, but He has not left us alone. He protects us and assures our ultimate safety with Him.

WHAT DOES THE BIBLE SAY?

John 10:7-15,27-30

7 So Jesus said again, "I assure you: I am the door of the sheep.
8 All who came before Me are thieves and robbers, but the sheep didn't listen to them. 9 I am the door. If anyone enters by Me, he will be saved and will come in and go out and find pasture.
10 A thief comes only to steal and to kill and to destroy. I have come so that they may have life and have it in abundance.

11 "I am the good shepherd. The good shepherd lays down his life for the sheep. 12 The hired man, since he is not the shepherd and doesn't own the sheep, leaves them and runs away when he sees a wolf coming. The wolf then snatches and scatters them. 13 This happens because he is a hired man and doesn't care about the sheep.

14 "I am the good shepherd. I know My own sheep, and they know Me, 15 as the Father knows Me, and I know the Father. I lay down My life for the sheep."

27 "My sheep hear My voice, I know them, and they follow Me.
28 I give them eternal life, and they will never perish—ever! No one will snatch them out of My hand. 29 My Father, who has given them to Me, is greater than all. No one is able to snatch them out of the Father's hand. 30 The Father and I are one."

The door of the sheep (v. 7)—A shepherd corralled sheep into makeshift pens at night for protection, forming a door with a bundle of sticks or his own person.

Abundance (v. 10)— The Greek word carries the connotation of super abundant or exceedingly abundant, well beyond the minimum. It can refer to both quality and quantity.

John 10:7-10

When Jesus announced, "I am the door of the sheep" (v. 7), He meant He was the *only* door for the sheep. He was claiming an exclusive status as Savior of the world—a claim that is repeated throughout the New Testament (see John 14:6 and Acts 4:12). While some chafe at this claim and try to soften it, there are no alternative meanings for Jesus' words. Jesus is not *one* way to God, He is *the only* way.

Jesus based His illustration on a sheep pen with a gate, not a closed room with a door (as our culture would think of a door). The only way to legitimately enter a sheep pen is through the door or gate. Since the sheep pen symbolizes a relationship with God, it follows that Jesus, the Door, is the only way to enter that relationship. Trusting in anything else—good works, religious tradition, the faith of others, and so on—will not give you access to a relationship with God. You must trust in Jesus alone.

Jesus warned about people who would distract His sheep from following Him. He said, "All who came before Me are thieves and robbers" (v. 8). Jesus was referring to religious leaders, such as the Pharisees and Sadducees, who were more interested in personal gain than in leading people to God. In very strong language, Jesus condemned anyone who interferes with people coming to Him.

Yet Jesus' words were not all negative. He also gave two wonderful promises:

▶ Anyone who follows Christ "will come in and go out and find pasture" (v. 9).

▶ "I have come so that they may have life and have it in abundance" (v. 10).

Jesus' followers move freely through life enjoying His blessings. We are promised abundant life—the opportunity to live life to the fullest.

Modern advertisers promise you can "have it all," but they lie. You can never get what you need through the products they advertise. Jesus promised you would have everything you need in life for true contentment and fulfillment—but only in Him. Jesus has given you more than you deserve and all of what truly matters in life.

> **Where do we encounter "thieves and robbers" in today's world?**

QUESTION #2

THE GOOD SHEPHERD

Read Psalm 23, below. In the space to the right, record at least one insight this psalm teaches you about God's character and care for His people.

¹ *The LORD is my shepherd;*
there is nothing I lack.
² *He lets me lie down*
in green pastures;
He leads me beside
quiet waters.
³ *He renews my life;*
He leads me along
the right paths
for His name's sake.
⁴ *Even when I go through*
the darkest valley,
I fear no danger,
for You are with me;
Your rod and Your staff—
they comfort me.
⁵ *You prepare a table*
before me
in the presence of
my enemies;
You anoint my head with oil;
my cup overflows.
⁶ *Only goodness and faithful*
love will pursue me
all the days of my life,
and I will dwell in the house
of the LORD
as long as I live.

John 10:11-13

Jesus made another significant "I am" statement in verse 11: "I am the good shepherd." Every shepherd does good for his sheep—leading them to pastures, protecting them from predators, tending to them when they're sick, and so forth. Jesus' listeners would have expected this, but He claimed much more. He described the good shepherd as one who "lays down His life for the sheep" (v. 11). Jesus does more than care for His sheep; He died for them.

Unfortunately, Jesus also highlighted two kinds of enemies who can limit people from establishing a relationship with God:

1. **The hired man.** Since he doesn't own the sheep, the hired man leaves them and runs away when trouble comes.

2. **A wolf.** The wolf "snatches and scatters" the sheep as an intentional act of destruction.

One enemy abandons the sheep when trouble comes; the other is the trouble. The Pharisees who heard these words likely cringed at the comparison. Jesus earlier had compared them to "thieves and robbers" (v. 8), and now to hirelings and wolves. Jesus minced no words in describing the damage religious leaders do when they are more concerned about preserving their traditions than introducing people to Christ.

Jesus' condemnation extends to any person—even a simple church member—who puts religious traditions and preferences ahead of helping people find their way to Him. It's easy to lose spiritual focus and think the church exists to meet our needs. It's dangerous to think our ways of doing things are the only acceptable choices and our preferences are best for everyone.

That's what the Pharisees did, and it can happen to us as well.

> **What do these "I am" statements teach us about Jesus' nature and character?**
>
> QUESTION #3

> **What makes Christians question their security in Christ?**

QUESTION **#4**

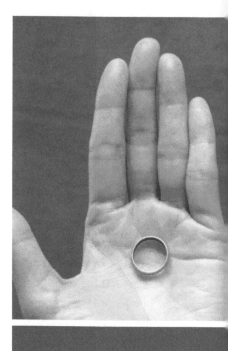

John 10:14-15,27-30

Jesus' care for His people (His sheep) is comprehensive and irrevocable. He promised that when He gives eternal life, His followers "will never perish—ever!" (v. 28). He used a two-fisted example to demonstrate what He meant. Jesus said of His followers, "No one will snatch them out of My hand" (v. 28) and "No one is able to snatch them out of the Father's hand" (v. 29).

As a young Christian, the fact that Jesus held me securely was difficult for me to believe. My mistake was assuming my efforts secured my relationship with God. While talking with a youth pastor and another friend about this, the pastor took off his wedding ring and handed it to my friend. He told him to make a fist around the ring and then wrap his free hand around his fist. Then the pastor put both his hands around my friend's hands. My youth pastor turned to me and said, "Try to get the wedding ring out of our hands."

Obviously, I couldn't do it. Then he said: "Jeff, Jesus has hold of you. God has hold of Jesus. You are completely secure. You are like the wedding ring; nothing can get to you."

That illustration isn't perfect, but it has stuck with me over the years. We are far more secure than that wedding ring. Once you establish a relationship with Jesus through faith, you belong to Him completely and permanently. No attack can defeat you, no sin can disqualify you, and no person can steal you away from Christ (see Rom. 8:31-39).

> **What's our role in accessing and benefiting from Jesus' protection?**

QUESTION **#5**

LIVE IT OUT

How will you respond this week to the offer of Jesus' protection? Consider the following options:

▶ **Identify your fears.** Be especially aware this week of circumstances that cause you to experience fear or concern. Record those moments in a journal or list, and use them as a starting point for prayer.

▶ **Study Christ.** Read more about the relationship between Jesus and the Father. See page 56 for a short description of what we know about God, and invest time in reading the Scriptures provided.

▶ **Share what you've learned.** Be intentional about sharing how Jesus has calmed your fears with someone who needs to hear it this week. Pray that God would provide opportunities and conversations that open the door for you to share what you've learned.

When fear arises, remember your security is in Jesus. He and the Father have you in a double-fisted handful of protective custody. Nothing can pluck you from Their hands!

My thoughts

OUR NEED FOR HOPE

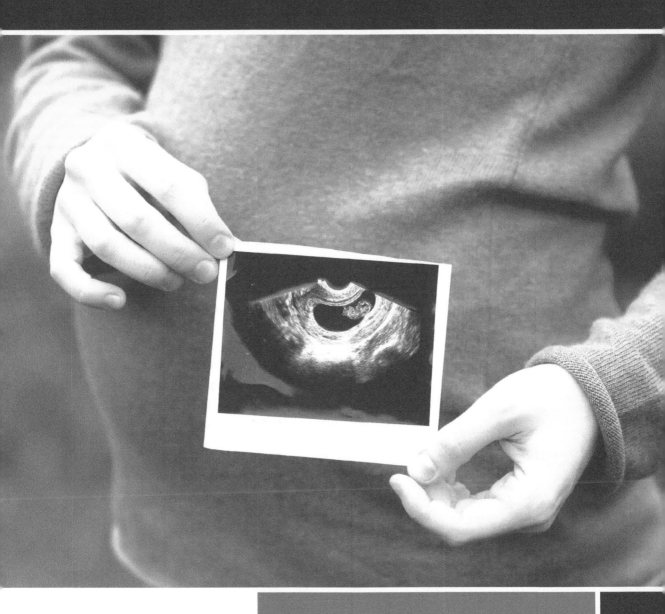

*What helps you feel hopeful
about the future?*

QUESTION #1

Jesus is the Resurrection who gives us life now and forever.

THE BIBLE MEETS LIFE

It happens every April. Thousands of baseball fans tell themselves, "This is the year my team wins the pennant!" Within a matter of months, however, the number of fans who hang on to that optimism will be slashed.

But they'll all be back again next year! To borrow from Alexander Pope, "Hope springs eternal."

Faltering hope is far more serious in other areas of life. For example, when someone dies whom we deeply love or on whom we've depended, we may feel we've lost all hope. Or, when cancer comes to our own door, we can become paralyzed with hopelessness.

These situations may seem hopeless, but Jesus' resurrection provides hope for ultimate victory—victory over death. While death is inevitable, it doesn't have to be our final reality. We can live again; we can experience an abundant life forever.

Jesus shows us how.

WHAT DOES THE BIBLE SAY?

John 11:17-27

17 When Jesus arrived, He found that Lazarus had already been in the tomb four days.

18 Bethany was near Jerusalem (about two miles away).

19 Many of the Jews had come to Martha and Mary to comfort them about their brother.

20 As soon as Martha heard that Jesus was coming, she went to meet Him. But Mary remained seated in the house.

21 Then Martha said to Jesus, "Lord, if You had been here, my brother wouldn't have died.

22 Yet even now I know that whatever You ask from God, God will give You."

23 "Your brother will rise again," Jesus told her.

24 Martha said, "I know that he will rise again in the resurrection at the last day."

25 Jesus said to her, "I am the resurrection and the life. The one who believes in Me, even if he dies, will live.

26 Everyone who lives and believes in Me will never die—ever. Do you believe this?"

27 "Yes, Lord," she told Him, "I believe You are the Messiah, the Son of God, who comes into the world."

Believe (v. 26)—This term means to entrust oneself to something, not just to assent to a mental proposition. Such belief is a process that assumes action will result and all of life will be affected.

The Messiah (v. 27)—The Anointed One God promised in the Old Testament who would come in the future and be instrumental in inaugurating the kingdom of God.

John 11:17-24

Lazarus had been sick. His sisters, Mary and Martha, were devoted followers of Jesus, so they sent a message to Him, hoping for a miraculous cure. Jesus delayed in coming, however, only arriving after Lazarus had "been in the tomb four days" (v. 17). The time frame is significant because Jewish folklore claimed a person's spirit hovered around the body for three days before departing for the afterlife. Therefore, anything Jesus did after arriving would be recognized as truly miraculous.

When Martha reached Jesus, she said, "Lord, if You had been here, my brother wouldn't have died" (v. 21). Her statement may sound like a rebuke, but her next statement helps us understand what she meant: "Yet even now I know that whatever You ask from God, God will give You" (v. 22). Martha's initial words were more a statement of fact than a rebuke. She said, in essence, "I know you have power over disease, and if you had arrived in time I know you could have healed my brother."

In response to Martha's comments, Jesus bluntly predicted, "Your brother will rise again" (v. 23).

This should have been shocking to Martha, but she took it in stride. That's because she heard Jesus' words in the context of the common doctrine taught by the Pharisees of her day. Martha believed in a generic resurrection at a future point in time—"at the last day" (v. 24)—when God would reveal His power over death. She had no real expectation Jesus would do anything more to help Lazarus.

In a sense, Martha's beliefs about the afterlife could be boiled down to the simple idea that, at some point in the future, everything would work out for the best. This notion is similar to what the majority of people believe about the afterlife today. Most people in our culture hope for some sort of life after death—some kind of heaven. This is a generic hope grounded more in a human sense of right and wrong (and in an overall positive outlook on life) than in God's Word. Sadly, this kind of generic, "don't worry, be happy" universalism is without substance. It brings false hope, which really is no hope at all.

Jesus has something better in mind for His followers. He has something better in mind for you!

> **What do our responses to tragedy reveal about our expectations of God?**
>
> QUESTION #2

THE HOPE OF HEAVEN

Which of the following images best represents what you hope to experience in heaven?

In what ways have you already experienced the blessings of eternal life in Christ?

John 11:25-26a

In verse 25, Jesus made His boldest and most direct claim about His power over life and death: "I am the resurrection and the life." This is the fifth of Jesus' seven "I am" statements in the Gospel of John.

1. **"I am the resurrection."** Jesus did not say, "I can resurrect someone." He said, "I *am* the resurrection." He overcame death by going through it Himself and coming out alive on the other side.

2. **"I am … the life."** Jesus established His power to give life—not just quantity of life (forever), but quality of life (full and meaningful life now and forever).

Jesus said the means to access both resurrection and life is to believe in Him. "The one who believes in Me, even if he dies, will live" (v. 25). Jesus challenged us to believe in Him personally as the means to eternal life—both now and forever. We must place our faith in Him alone. Mental agreement isn't enough. There is no substitute for personal faith. You must *believe* in Jesus!

We often express personal faith in a prayer of commitment. If you are willing to place total trust in Jesus, then tell Him so honestly and earnestly in prayer.

Jesus continued with a statement that almost sounds contradictory: "Everyone who lives and believes in Me will never die—ever" (v. 26). The wonderful promise from Jesus' words is that physical death does not prevent us from experiencing eternal life. Life for the follower of Christ continues—even after physical death—in a glorified, resurrected body (see 1 Cor. 15:35-57). When you believe in Jesus, you get the best in both worlds. You have meaningful life now and eternal life with Him forever.

> *What does this "I am" statement teach us about Jesus' nature and character?*
>
> QUESTION **#3**

> *How does Jesus' statement in these verses produce hope?*
>
> QUESTION **#4**

"Death used to be an executioner, but the gospel has made him just a gardener."

—GEORGE HERBERT

John 11:26b-27

Jesus asked Martha a direct question: "Do you believe this?" (v. 26). He wanted a straight answer to an honest question based on what He had just revealed. He wants the same from us, as well.

In the next scene of this story, Jesus—along with Mary and Martha and many of the other mourners—arrived at Lazarus's grave. Jesus was about to provide the ultimate object lesson to support His statement about being the resurrection and the life. At the tomb, He said, "Remove the stone" (v. 39).

Martha's response was eminently practical: "Lord, he's already decaying. It's been four days" (v. 39). Did this statement mean Martha lacked faith? No. She only lacked understanding. Her words expressed what everyone standing in front of that tomb must have been thinking: "It's way too late for what Jesus does—heal the sick."

Jesus had something different in mind. He was moving beyond healing the sick to resuscitating the dead. (A resuscitated person ultimately dies again; a resurrected person never dies.) When Jesus resuscitated Lazarus, it served as a miraculous object lesson to demonstrate His own future resurrection, and the resurrection awaiting every person who believes in Him.

Jesus brought Lazarus out of the grave with the power of His voice. He has the power to give life and to sustain it—even through death. Jesus is your Source of life, both now and forever.

> *How does the hope of eternal life influence your daily decisions?*

QUESTION #5

LIVE **IT OUT**

Jesus is the resurrection and the life. Consider the following options for putting that truth into practice this week:

▶ **Answer the question.** Take some time to reflect on Jesus' question to Martha regarding His claim to be the resurrection and the life: "Do you believe this?" Answer that question for your own life.

▶ **Pray.** Make a list of people within your spheres of influence who have not expressed faith in Jesus. Pray daily for each of those individuals by name.

▶ **Initiate a conversation.** In addition to praying for those who need to experience Jesus as the resurrection and the life, take the next step of initiating a spiritual conversation with someone on that list. Express what you've experienced in your time as a follower of Christ, and express your desire to see that person know Christ, as well.

This may not be the year your favorite team wins a championship. But it can be the year you experience Jesus' resurrection power in a deeper and more meaningful way. Take the steps necessary to know where you stand with Christ—and to help others encounter the One who offers life both now and forever.

My thoughts

OUR NEED FOR PEACE

When have you felt most at peace?

Jesus is the way to the Father; therefore, we can live in peace.

THE BIBLE MEETS LIFE

Atticus Finch, the small-town Alabama lawyer in Harper Lee's *To Kill a Mockingbird*, is one of the most beloved characters in American literature. Throughout the novel, Atticus maintains a calm poise in all situations—whether facing down a rabid dog or dealing with a racially-motivated mob. Several times in the narrative, Atticus tells his children, Jem and Scout, "It's not time to worry." Atticus is always very open with his children, so they trust that if there ever *is* a time to worry, he'll tell them.

Trouble has a way of finding us, and it's easy to let those troubles cause us to worry. It would be nice to have our own version of Atticus Finch—someone to tell us, "It's not time to worry."

The truth is that we don't need a fictitious character like Atticus. We have Jesus, who offers us something far greater. He doesn't just offer words in an attempt to comfort us; He offers Himself. Jesus does what no Atticus Finch could ever do: He gives us true peace even in the midst of trouble.

Universal / The Kobal Collection

WHAT DOES THE BIBLE SAY?

John 14:1-7

1 "Your heart must not be troubled. Believe in God; believe also in Me.

2 In My Father's house are many dwelling places; if not, I would have told you. I am going away to prepare a place for you.

3 If I go away and prepare a place for you, I will come back and receive you to Myself, so that where I am you may be also.

4 You know the way to where I am going."

5 "Lord," Thomas said, "we don't know where You're going. How can we know the way?"

6 Jesus told him, "I am the way, the truth, and the life. No one comes to the Father except through Me.

7 "If you know Me, you will also know My Father. From now on you do know Him and have seen Him."

Troubled (v. 1)—Can refer to outward shaking or stirring up; or inward turmoil, unsettling circumstances, or being thrown into confusion.

Dwelling places (v. 2)—Place of remaining, tarrying, staying, or dwelling, as in a room or abode, or even of a settled residence.

Know (v. 7)—All three uses in this verse come from the Greek word meaning "to know by personal experience." A different Greek word appears in verses 4-5.

> **How do you determine if someone is trustworthy?**

QUESTION **#2**

John 14:1

"Your heart must not be troubled." It was just hours before His arrest, trial, and crucifixion, yet Jesus was not focused on Himself. Rather, He sought to comfort and encourage His disciples. These men had already experienced difficulty because of their commitment to Him. Jesus knew it was going to get worse—much worse. Persecution was coming. Martyrdom would soon be a reality.

Becoming a Christian has never been an escape hatch from trouble. Our faith often invites conflict. And believers experience many of the same difficulties in life as unbelievers: sickness, accidents, natural disasters, crimes, wars, and much more. We are not exempt from the results of sin's curse on our world. Believers must also go through the trial of physical death—often after enduring declining health, loss of mental faculties, and loneliness leading to depression.

For all these reasons, Jesus knew finding and maintaining peace would be difficult. His encouragement, "Your heart must not be troubled," advocates a practical reality, not a theoretical possibility.

Maybe you're wondering, *How exactly am I supposed to avoid being overcome by trouble?*

Jesus revealed the Source of peace in the midst of trouble: "Believe in God; believe also in Me." The word "believe" in this context also could be translated "trust." The key is trusting God and Jesus to sustain you through whatever challenges come your way.

Notice that Jesus didn't say simply to trust the *power* of God or the *presence* of Jesus. Instead, this is a trust based on a relationship with God that is personal and intimate. We trust in Persons, not merely in concepts or doctrines. That is a distinctive element of the Christian faith.

Several years ago, after being diagnosed with cancer, I had two surgeries in five days. The night after the second surgery was very difficult. During the night, I became desperate for help. My prayer was, "God, just get me through to the morning." All my education and experiences were useless. I had no strength of my own. That night, it was just me trusting God—and He was enough.

When you face real trouble, trust God and discover the sustaining grace He provides.

PERSONAL ASSESSMENT: PEACE

Are you a peaceful person? Use the following evaluations as a starting point to find out. To what degree do you feel at peace in these areas of life?

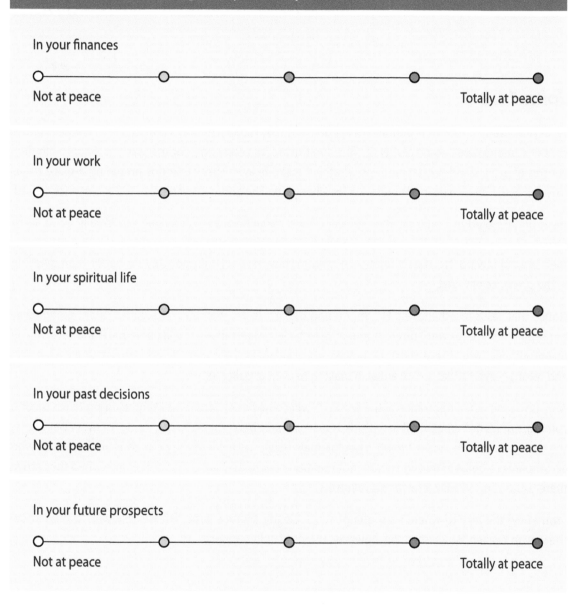

In your finances

Not at peace   Totally at peace

In your work

Not at peace   Totally at peace

In your spiritual life

Not at peace   Totally at peace

In your past decisions

Not at peace   Totally at peace

In your future prospects

Not at peace   Totally at peace

> *What do you find most comforting in these verses? Why?*

QUESTION **#3**

John 14:2-4

Jesus promised His followers permanent residence in His "Father's house." He also said His Father's house contains "many dwelling places" (v. 2). But don't fixate on receiving your mansion, as if some glorified version of a brick-and-mortar castle is what will make heaven special. God is preparing a place for us to dwell *with Him*—to be in His presence for all eternity. The grandeur of heaven is the presence of God!

Jesus underscored this priority when He said, "I will come back and receive you to Myself" (v. 3). Jesus promised to retrieve His followers, accompany them beyond death, and bring them into His presence as their eternal reward. No stately home—no matter how nice—could possibly be better than dwelling in the presence of Christ.

Notice that Jesus foreshadowed His impending departure. He warned His disciples, "I am going away to prepare a place for you," but in the next breath He assured them, "I will come back and receive you to Myself" (vv. 2-3). These short sentences summarize His upcoming death, resurrection, ascension, and return—events that are essential in making heaven a reality for us.

Also, don't miss the importance of the words, "I will come back." Jesus was likely referring to His second coming, but it's not unreasonable to think Jesus may have been speaking of coming for every believer at the moment of death. Again, timing is not the main issue. The focus of the promise is on the Person who accompanies a believer through death, not the place where they are going or the time when they arrive there. Jesus Himself will come for His followers.

"You know the way to where I am going" (v. 4). Clearly, by now Jesus felt His followers should know the way to heaven. As we shall see, however, they still didn't understand.

John 14:5-7

Confused about Jesus' earlier statement, Thomas responded honestly: "We don't know where You're going. How can we know the way?" (v. 5). Jesus' answer included no hint of rebuke; instead, He offered one of His most powerful and concise statements: "I am the way, the truth, and the life. No one comes to the Father except through Me" (v. 6).

Jesus didn't say He was a source or teacher of the way; He said, "*I am* the way." Our faith is personal—it's generated by a Person and accessed through a relationship with a Person. Similarly, while Jesus taught truth and gave life, He claimed to be more than a source for these things. Jesus *is* truth and life.

Jesus' claim to being the way, truth, and life may be the clearest example in Scripture about the exclusivity of the gospel. We find absolutely no biblical foundation for universalism—the misguided belief that all faiths are equal and all roads lead to heaven. Jesus is the only way, the only truth, and the only life.

Today, an ever-growing number of people are uncomfortable with the implications of this claim. It might seem the solution is to appease critics by softening Jesus' words—not only about salvation, but also about sexuality, morality, ethics, and integrity. Rather than trying to soften those words, let's take them seriously. Let them motivate our witness, deepen our spiritual resolve, and increase our efforts to get the gospel to more people. That's the best response to Jesus' definitive words, and the only way to true peace.

> *What does this "I am" statement teach us about Jesus' nature and character?*

QUESTION **#4**

> *Why is lasting peace found only in Jesus?*

QUESTION **#5**

LIVE IT OUT

Jesus is our only Source of true peace during difficulty. Consider the following options for helping others experience this hope:

▶ **Praise God.** Spend an hour thanking Jesus for the place He has prepared for you in heaven. Praise God for blessing you with peace and an eternal home with Christ.

▶ **Memorize the Word.** Work each day to commit John 14:6 to memory. Encourage friends and family members to join you in memorizing this important verse.

▶ **Be bold.** Invite a person of a different faith to coffee or lunch. Ask this person to explain what his or her religion teaches about concepts like the way to heaven, truth, and eternal life. In turn, share what Jesus taught and what you believe about these issues.

There are times when all of us worry in this world. Even Atticus Finch felt the pressure of those moments. But you have the amazing gift of choosing to focus on Christ in even the worst of moments—and in doing so, you'll find the gift of peace.

My *thoughts*

OUR NEED FOR PURPOSE

When have you felt like a hamster on a wheel?

QUESTION *#1*

Jesus is the Vine who empowers us to live productive lives for God.

THE BIBLE MEETS LIFE

"I'm *sooo* busy." We hear that a lot, don't we? Some people say it with a sigh, but they may also betray a hint of pride. Being busy is a badge of honor in our society. It can be a way to convince ourselves we are significant and important.

It also can present a problem. Why? Because busyness does not equal productivity.

The truth is that we never find ultimate purpose in what we do. Purpose is more personal. Finding purpose is about knowing a Person and allowing Him to shape our lives. Real life—deep, meaningful, satisfying life—comes from connecting to Jesus and allowing His life to flow through ours.

On the surface, that may sound syrupy and spiritual—completely out of touch with the rough-and-tumble daily life of the real world. But Jesus made the concept very practical, and He did it by talking about a vineyard.

WHAT DOES THE BIBLE SAY?

John 15:1-8

1 "I am the true vine, and My Father is the vineyard keeper.

2 Every branch in Me that does not produce fruit He removes, and He prunes every branch that produces fruit so that it will produce more fruit.

3 You are already clean because of the word I have spoken to you.

4 Remain in Me, and I in you. Just as a branch is unable to produce fruit by itself unless it remains on the vine, so neither can you unless you remain in Me.

5 "I am the vine; you are the branches. The one who remains in Me and I in him produces much fruit, because you can do nothing without Me.

6 If anyone does not remain in Me, he is thrown aside like a branch and he withers. They gather them, throw them into the fire, and they are burned.

7 If you remain in Me and My words remain in you, ask whatever you want and it will be done for you.

8 My Father is glorified by this: that you produce much fruit and prove to be My disciples."

Remain (v. 4)—This term refers to existing in a specific state or condition for an extended period of time; in this case, remaining in the presence of Jesus.

Glorified (v. 8)—Enhanced reputation, praise, or honor of someone or something; to achieve splendid greatness in one's person, possessions, or circumstances in the opinion of others.

> **What does this "I am" statement teach us about Jesus' nature and character?**

QUESTION #2

John 15:1-3

Only hours before His arrest and crucifixion, Jesus made His seventh "I am" statement. By calling Himself the True Vine, Jesus established Himself as the Source of all that flows from Him to His followers. Since He is the Source of life for every branch (His followers), it is critical that the branches are vitally and solidly connected to Him.

Jesus announced the Vineyard Keeper (God) would remove every branch that doesn't produce fruit—meaning, visible evidence of a living connection to the vine. People who falsely claim to be followers of Jesus are unmasked by their lack of spiritual fruit. As a result of their counterfeit faith, God removes them from their pseudo-relationship with Christ.

It all comes down to a matter of spiritual fruit. But what kind of fruit is this?

1. Some people equate fruit with evangelistic success, meaning how many people you lead to faith in Jesus.

2. Some people connect fruit to acts of service, meaning the ministry you do in the name of Jesus.

3. Some people insist fruit is about personal growth—the character of Jesus that God shapes in you.

All of these views are correct. Life change must happen—and continue to happen—as proof of conversion. Yet, to bear fruit can mean leading people to Jesus (see John 4:36), serving them in Jesus' name (see Matt. 7:16-20), *and* developing the character of Christ (see Gal. 5:22-23).

God also "prunes every branch that produces fruit so that it will produce more fruit" (v. 2). Pruning applies to those who have proven the legitimacy of their faith. God continually works to produce spiritual fruit among Jesus' followers. God is unrelenting in shaping His people to be more and more like Jesus.

Such pruning can be painful, but it's good. Change that brings us closer to Christ is always good. So ask yourself: *Am I changing to be more like Jesus?* Progress, not perfection, is the goal.

ABIDE IN CHRIST

What steps will you take to remain in Christ this week? Use the following acrostic to help identify specific ways you can focus on your relationship with Him. (An example is provided to get you started.)

A

Read the **B**ible each day.

I

D

E

John 15:4-7

What does "remaining in Christ" look like in our daily lives?

QUESTION **#3**

Jesus used one word repeatedly in this passage: "remain." In fact, He used it 10 times throughout John 15:4-10. Jesus wanted to emphasize the mutual interweaving of His life with the lives of His followers.

To "remain" in this context carries the idea of personal, intimate residence. Jesus emphasized that His followers must abide in Him, and He in them. The intricacy and interconnectedness of the relationship between Jesus and His followers is difficult to express—and impossible to overstate!

Jesus also included a warning: "If anyone does not remain in Me, he is thrown aside like a branch and he withers" (v. 6). If half-hearted believers fail to live in Jesus and produce fruit, not only will they be removed (see v. 2), but they will also face destruction.

In stark contrast to the calamity awaiting false believers, true believers have fantastic privileges—including unlimited access to God in prayer. Jesus promised, "If you remain in Me and My words remain in you, ask whatever you want and it will be done for you" (v. 7).

When you remain in Christ, your thoughts are saturated with the mind of Jesus, your heart beats with the compassion of Jesus, and your will bows to the Lordship of Jesus—all of which changes your prayers. Rather than praying a laundry list of self-serving demands, the believer who remains in Jesus will pray like Jesus prays:

How would you summarize the commands and promises in these verses?

QUESTION **#4**

1. Humble yourself.

2. Meditate on God's Word.

3. Consider what Jesus would pray in your situation.

4. Then go ahead, pray boldly!

You can trust you'll receive God's best answer in His good time.

John 15:8

Bringing glory to God is the goal for every believer.

To glorify God means to make His name famous, give Him the accolades, and put Him on prominent display. We can glorify God in two ways:

1. **You glorify God when you "produce much fruit."** When you lead people to faith, accomplish difficult ministry and service, or overcome ingrained personal weaknesses, people will notice. And when you humbly acknowledge your inability to generate any of these accomplishments on your own and point to God, He gets the glory.

2. **You glorify God when you "prove to be My disciples."** No one can generate genuine life change on their own. Therefore, changes in you will point to Someone beyond you—to God.

Purpose is found when you step off the ugly treadmill of duty-bound religious busyness and get on the slow-but-sure track toward bearing fruit for Christ. Commit yourself to Jesus for strength to tackle day-to-day living. Allow His grace to flow through you. Revel in His love. When you do these things, your efforts to serve and grow will flow freely, and you will bear much fruit for Him.

A life in Christ is a productive life. It's a life with purpose.

"Give me a man who says,
'This one thing I do,' and not,
'These 50 things I dabble in.'"

—D.L. MOODY

LIVE IT OUT

What steps will you take this week to remain in Jesus, the Vine? Consider the following options:

▶ **Double down.** Each day this week, spend twice as much time praying and reading God's Word as you usually do. Take an active step to remain in Christ.

▶ **Say thanks.** Consider one way God has changed you or used you in recent months. Write a "thank you" letter to God giving Him the glory for the fruit in your life. Consider sharing your letter with those close to you.

▶ **Plan ahead.** Review your monthly calendar and eliminate any activities that won't bring glory to God. Modify or replace other activities so they can be done in Christ's power and bring glory to Him.

Even on your busiest day, remember that Jesus alone is your Source for purpose in this life. Choose to remain in Him and allow His power to produce fruit for His glory.

My group's prayer requests

....

....

....

....

....

....

....

....

....

....

....

My thoughts

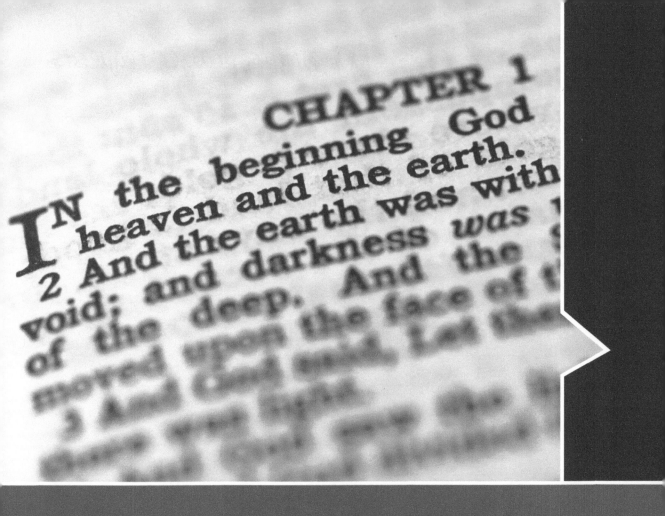

WHAT WE KNOW ABOUT GOD

EXCERPTED FROM *THE BAPTIST FAITH AND MESSAGE*

There is one and only one living and true God. He is an intelligent, spiritual, and personal Being, the Creator, Redeemer, Preserver, and Ruler of the universe. God is infinite in holiness and all other perfections. God is all powerful and all knowing; and His perfect knowledge extends to all things, past, present, and future, including the future decisions of His free creatures. To Him we owe the highest love, reverence, and obedience. The eternal triune God reveals Himself to us as Father, Son, and Holy Spirit, with distinct personal attributes, but without division of nature, essence, or being.

God the Father

God as Father reigns with providential care over His universe, His creatures, and the flow of the stream of human history according to the purposes of His grace. He is all powerful, all knowing, all loving, and all wise.

God is Father in truth to those who become children of God through faith in Jesus Christ. He is fatherly in His attitude toward all men.

Scripture support: Genesis 1:1; 2:7; Exodus 3:14; 6:2-3; 15:11ff.; 20:1ff.; Leviticus 22:2; Deuteronomy 6:4; 32:6; 1 Chronicles 29:10; Psalm 19:1-3; Isaiah 43:3,15; 64:8; Jeremiah 10:10; 17:13; Matthew 6:9ff.; 7:11; 23:9; 28:19; Mark 1:9-11; John 4:24; 5:26; 14:6-13; 17:1-8; Acts 1:7; Romans 8:14-15; 1 Corinthians 8:6; Galatians 4:6; Ephesians 4:6; Colossians 1:15; 1 Timothy 1:17; Hebrews 11:6; 12:9; 1 Peter 1:17; 1 John 5:7.

God the Son

Christ is the eternal Son of God. In His incarnation as Jesus Christ He was conceived of the Holy Spirit and born of the virgin Mary.

Jesus perfectly revealed and did the will of God, taking upon Himself human nature with its demands and necessities and identifying Himself completely with mankind yet without sin. He honored the divine law by His personal obedience, and in His substitutionary death on the cross He made provision for the redemption of men from sin.

He was raised from the dead with a glorified body and appeared to His disciples as the person who was with them before His crucifixion.

He ascended into heaven and is now exalted at the right hand of God where He is the One Mediator, fully God, fully man, in whose Person is effected the reconciliation between God and man.

He will return in power and glory to judge the world and to consummate His redemptive mission. He now dwells in all believers as the living and ever present Lord.

Scripture support: Genesis 18:1ff.; Psalms 2:7ff.; 110:1ff.; Isaiah 7:14; 53; Matthew 1:18-23; 3:17; 8:29; 11:27; 14:33; 16:16,27; 17:5; 27; 28:1-6,19; Mark 1:1; 3:11; Luke 1:35; 4:41; 22:70; 24:46; John 1:1-18,29; 10:30,38; 11:25-27; 12:44-50; 14:7-11; 16:15-16,28; 17:1-5, 21-22; 20:1-20,28; Acts 1:9; 2:22-24; 7:55-56; 9:4-5,20; Romans 1:3-4; 3:23-26; 5:6-21; 8:1-3,34; 10:4; 1 Corinthians 1:30; 2:2; 8:6; 15:1-8,24-28; 2 Corinthians 5:19-21; 8:9; Galatians 4:4-5; Ephesians 1:20; 3:11; 4:7-10; Philippians 2:5-11; Colossians 1:13-22; 2:9; 1 Thessalonians 4:14-18; 1 Timothy 2:5-6; 3:16; Titus 2:13-14; Hebrews 1:1-3; 4:14-15; 7:14-28; 9:12-15,24-28; 12:2; 13:8; 1 Peter 2:21-25; 3:22; 1 John 1:7-9; 3:2; 4:14-15; 5:9; 2 John 7-9; Revelation 1:13-16; 5:9-14; 12:10-11; 13:8; 19:16.

God the Holy Spirit

The Holy Spirit is the Spirit of God, fully divine. He inspired holy men of old to write the Scriptures. Through illumination He enables men to understand truth. He exalts Christ. He convicts men of sin, of righteousness, and of judgment. He calls men to the Savior, and effects regeneration. At the moment of regeneration He baptizes every believer into the Body of Christ.

He cultivates Christian character, comforts believers, and bestows the spiritual gifts by which they serve God through His church. He seals the believer unto the day of final redemption. His presence in the Christian is the guarantee that God will bring the believer into the fullness of the stature of Christ. He enlightens and empowers the believer and the church in worship, evangelism, and service.

Scripture support: Genesis 1:2; Judges 14:6; Job 26:13; Psalms 51:11; 139:7ff.; Isaiah 61:1-3; Joel 2:28-32; Matthew 1:18; 3:16; 4:1; 12:28-32; 28:19; Mark 1:10,12; Luke 1:35; 4:1,18-19; 11:13; 12:12; 24:49; John 4:24; 14:16-17,26; 15:26; 16:7-14; Acts 1:8; 2:1-4,38; 4:31; 5:3; 6:3; 7:55; 8:17,39; 10:44; 13:2; 15:28; 16:6; 19:1-6; Romans 8:9-11,14-16,26-27; 1 Corinthians 2:10-14; 3:16; 12:3-11,13; Galatians 4:6; Ephesians 1:13-14; 4:30; 5:18; 1 Thessalonians 5:19; 1 Timothy 3:16; 4:1; 2 Timothy 1:14; 3:16; Hebrews 9:8,14; 2 Peter 1:21; 1 John 4:13; 5:6-7; Revelation 1:10; 22:17.

This article has been excerpted from *The Baptist Faith and Message* (2000). Source: *sbc.net/bfm2000/bfm2000.asp.*

LEADER GUIDE | MORE THAN ENOUGH

GENERAL INSTRUCTIONS

In order to make the most of this study and to ensure a richer group experience, it's recommended that all group participants read through the teaching and discussion content in full before each group meeting. As a leader, it is also a good idea for you to be familiar with this content and prepared to summarize it for your group members as you move through the material each week.

Each session of the Bible study is made up of three sections:

1. THE BIBLE MEETS LIFE.

An introduction to the theme of the session and its connection to everyday life, along with a brief overview of the primary Scripture text. This section also includes an icebreaker question or activity.

2. WHAT DOES THE BIBLE SAY?

This comprises the bulk of each session and includes the primary Scripture text along with explanations for key words and ideas within that text. This section also includes most of the content designed to produce and maintain discussion within the group.

3. LIVE IT OUT.

The final section focuses on application, using bulleted summary statements to answer the question, *So what?* As the leader, be prepared to challenge the group to apply what they learned during the discussion by transforming it into action throughout the week.

For group leaders, this *More than Enough* leader guide contains several features and tools designed to help you lead participants through the material provided.

QUESTION 1—ICEBREAKER

These opening questions and/or activities are designed to help participants transition into the study and begin engaging the primary themes to be discussed. Be sure everyone has a chance to speak, but maintain a low-pressure environment.

DISCUSSION QUESTIONS

Each "What Does the Bible Say?" section features six questions designed to spark discussion and interaction in your group. These questions encourage critical thinking, so be sure to allow a period of silence for participants to process the question and form an answer.

The *More than Enough* leader guide also contains follow-up questions and optional activities that may be helpful to your group, if time permits.

DVD CONTENT

Each video features Jeff Iorg discussing the primary themes found in the session. We recommend you show this video in one of three places: (1) At the beginning of the group time, (2) After the icebreaker, or (3) After a quick review and/or summary of "What Does the Bible Say?" A video summary is included as well. You may choose to use this summary as background preparation to help you guide the group.

The leader guide contains additional questions to help unpack the video and transition into the discussion. For a digital leader guide with commentary, see the "Leader Tools" folder on the DVD-ROM in your Bible study kit.

For helps on how to use *Bible Studies for Life,* tips on how to better lead groups, or additional ideas for leading, visit *ministrygrid.com/web/BibleStudiesforLife.*

SESSION 1: OUR NEED FOR CONTENTMENT

The Point: Jesus is the Bread of life who gives us true satisfaction.

The Passage: John 6:26-27,35-40

The Setting: John 6 opens with Jesus feeding the 5,000 (though that number refers only to the men present, not including the women and children). That multiplying of food, coupled with earlier healing works Jesus had performed, had the crowds ready "to make Him king" (v. 15). Jesus and the disciples departed that evening. The next day, the crowds, still exhilarated over the free feast, came looking for Jesus (see vv. 22-25).

QUESTION 1: When have you recently had too much of a good thing?

> *Optional activity:* Supplement question 1 by providing group members with a "good thing" of some kind. This could be a snack or other food item; it could also be a small gift, a note of encouragement, and so on. Once group members have had enough of this good thing, transition to talk about a recent experience when they had too much of a good thing.

Video Summary: In John 6:35, Jesus said, "I am the bread of life." He is our sustenance, provision, and comfort. He provides for us both permanently and perpetually. How do we access Jesus as the Bread of life? Not through our works. Not by trying to prove ourselves. We simply believe in Him. Security as believers isn't something we get when we die. It's something we have from the moment we believe. Jesus can meet our needs now, and He can meet our needs in the future.

▶ WATCH THE DVD SEGMENT FOR SESSION 1. THEN USE THE FOLLOWING QUESTIONS AND DISCUSSION POINTS TO TRANSITION INTO THE STUDY.

● In his video message Jeff says, "All that Jesus has done in your past is a reminder that He can meet your needs now and into the future—no matter what they are." Share with your group a time in the past when Jesus provided for your needs.

● In what ways can you use reminders like this to help you trust God in the future? Be specific.

WHAT DOES THE BIBLE SAY?

▶ ASK FOR A VOLUNTEER TO READ ALOUD JOHN 6:26-27,35-40.

Response: What's your initial reaction to these verses?

● What do you like about the text?

● What questions do you have about these verses?

▶ TURN THE GROUP'S ATTENTION TO JOHN 6:26-27.

QUESTION 2: Why do people seek satisfaction in things that don't last?

Answering this question requires group members to examine the things in their own lives that have led them to seek satisfaction from the wrong sources. Remind them that they are not alone and encourage them in their honesty.

> *Optional follow-up:* What are some ways people seek satisfaction in today's culture?

▶ MOVE TO JOHN 6:35.

QUESTION 3: When have you experienced spiritual hunger or thirst?

This question provides group members with an opportunity to share a personal story based on their own life experiences.

> *Optional follow-up:* In what ways have you experienced those needs being met?

QUESTION 4: What does this "I am" statement teach us about Jesus' nature and character?

This question asks group members to interpret the biblical text in terms of what can be learned about Jesus from this passage about Jesus. Encourage them to look beyond the words.

> *Optional follow-up:* How would you explain the term "bread of life" to someone who's never heard it?

▶ CONTINUE WITH JOHN 6:36-40.

QUESTION 5: How would you describe your experiences with the bread of life?

Answers will vary as group members filter their responses through their own life experiences. This question provides an opportunity to interpret and internalize the biblical text as they share with the group.

> *Optional activity:* Direct group members to complete the activity "Meeting Needs" on page 13. As time permits, encourage group members to share how Christ has met different needs in their lives.

Note: The following question does not appear in the Bible study book. Use it in your group discussion as time allows.

QUESTION 6: What do these verses communicate about eternal life?

The intent of this question is to prompt interaction with the biblical text. Encourage group members to examine the passage closely.

LIVE IT OUT

Encourage group members to consider the following ways they can seek out greater contentment:

- **Give it up.** Identify something temporary you have been pursuing as a means of security—a possession, an achievement, an accomplishment, and so on. Stop your pursuit. Repent and ask God to grant you true contentment in Jesus.

- **Give thanks.** Commit to expressing gratitude this week when others serve or bless you. Thankfulness is a great way to avoid self-centeredness and promote satisfaction.

- **Give it away.** Volunteer with a ministry that serves others in need. While doing so, share the gospel with someone by using this Scripture passage to help him or her understand true satisfaction comes from Jesus Christ.

Challenge: So many people in our society are convinced that more is better, bigger is best, and getting our way equals prosperity and happiness. But satisfaction sought through this mindset is fleeting. Be on alert this week for people you encounter who are on this treadmill and be prepared to share with them where they can find true satisfaction.

Pray: Ask for prayer requests and ask group members to pray for the different requests as intercessors. As the leader, close this time by expressing your belief in Jesus as the Bread of life. On behalf of your group, thank Him for the privilege of never needing to be spiritually hungry or thirsty again.

SESSION 2: OUR NEED FOR DIRECTION

The Point: Jesus is the Light who reveals the way we should go.

The Passage: John 8:12-19

The Setting: Early excitement over Jesus and His miraculous works had begun to wane. His teachings had begun to challenge people's beliefs, and many ceased to be enamored with Him as He clarified who He was and what He had come to do. Included in His description of His character and nature was the fact that He is the Light of the world.

QUESTION 1: When do you remember feeling afraid of the dark?

> *Optional activity:* Help your group members appreciate Jesus' role as Light of the world by making your meeting space as dark as is reasonable while discussing question 1. Turn off the lights, use sheets to cover any windows, and so on.

> *Note:* If your group is meeting in a place where darkness isn't practical, consider seeking out an adjacent room or stairwell to discuss question 1—or ask group members to close their eyes.

Video Summary: In John 8:12 Jesus said, "I am the light of the world." Jesus was saying He is the source of salvation and direction. Worldly wisdom and cultural information often distract us. False information is available everywhere. We are bombarded by misinformation about life and our salvation. Our challenge is to set aside these distractions and find a way to hear what Jesus is saying to us about salvation and direction.

▶ WATCH THE DVD SEGMENT FOR SESSION 2. THEN USE THE FOLLOWING QUESTIONS AND DISCUSSION POINTS TO TRANSITION INTO THE STUDY.

- If Jesus is the source of salvation and direction, why do you think those things are sometimes so difficult to find?

- Jeff says, "We have a responsibility to discern whether the information we are receiving is a pure message about Jesus." In what ways can you go about doing that? Be specific with your responses.

WHAT DOES THE BIBLE SAY?

▶ ASK FOR A VOLUNTEER TO READ ALOUD JOHN 8:12-19.

Response: What's your initial reaction to these verses?

- What questions do you have about these verses?

- What do you hope to learn this week about how Jesus reveals the way we should go?

▶ TURN THE GROUP'S ATTENTION TO JOHN 8:12.

QUESTION 2: Where do you see evidence of darkness in today's world?

The intent of this question is to move group members from Scripture interpretation to life application. In doing so, they will be better able to identify specific instances of darkness in the world today.

> **Optional follow-up:** What is one area where you can shine the light of Jesus into the darkness? How will you do that?

QUESTION 3: What does this "I am" statement teach us about Jesus' nature and character?

This question asks group members to interpret the biblical text in terms of what can be learned from this passage about Jesus. Encourage them to look beyond the words.

> **Optional follow-up:** How has Jesus been the light throughout history?

▶ MOVE TO JOHN 8:13-15.

QUESTION 4: What are some reasons people give today for rejecting God's Word as truth?

This question is designed to lead group members to consider why people (themselves as well as others) tend to reject God's Word as truth. Answers will vary based on individual experiences.

> **Optional follow-up:** What are some symptoms of trying to blend God's truth with human standards?

> **Optional activity:** Direct group members to complete the activity "Your Testimony" on page 19. As time permits, encourage volunteers to share how they would testify about who Jesus is.

▶ CONTINUE WITH JOHN 8:16-19.

QUESTION 5: What decisions must we make in order to follow Jesus' judgments and directions?

Ask group members to work together to answer this question. By encouraging them to define practical and specific decisions, they will feel better prepared to follow Jesus' judgments and directions as individuals.

> **Optional follow-up:** What obstacles often prevent us from making those decisions (or from following through with the decisions we've made)?

Note: The following question does not appear in the Bible study book. Use it in your group discussion as time allows.

QUESTION 6: How has Jesus been the Light in your life?

This question gives group members an opportunity to consider for themselves and then share with the group how they have experienced Jesus as the Light in their lives through their own personal circumstances.

LIVE IT OUT

Since Jesus is the Light of the world, how will that truth influence your actions and attitudes this week? Invite group members to consider taking one of the following steps in response:

- **Identify.** Seek out an area of your life in which you are following sources of light other than Christ. Take action to move away from those sources and follow Christ.

- **Submit.** Begin each day this week by verbally submitting yourself to God. Proclaim your desire to walk only in the direction revealed by the light of Christ, and continually pray for guidance throughout the day.

- **Study.** Read a book on Christian worldview such as *Mere Christianity* by C. S. Lewis. If possible, study this book with someone else and discuss what it teaches about following the light and direction of Jesus.

Challenge: There will be times when you find yourself in darkness—our world is filled with it, after all. But you never have to be alone in that darkness. Are there people in your life you can call when you find yourself in the midst of darkness? If not, work on building a support system for when those times come.

Pray: Ask for prayer requests and ask group members to pray for the different requests as intercessors. As the leader, conclude by thanking Jesus for the many times He has provided necessary light for your life. On behalf of your group, proclaim your desire to reflect His light to a world and culture that is often filled with darkness.

The Point: Jesus is the only One who offers us ultimate protection.

The Passage: John 10:7-15,27-30

The Setting: The Hebrew people understood sheep, shepherds, and shepherding. Their great king, David, had been a shepherd, like many before and since. Their Scripture, our Old Testament, utilized the imagery of sheep and shepherd to depict the chosen people and God Himself. Religious leadership liked to fancy themselves as shepherds to the people, as well. Jesus understood, and set out to demonstrate, that the religious leaders were really strangers, not shepherds, who cared for the sheep.

QUESTION 1: When have you felt protected during a strange or scary situation?

> *Optional activity:* Complement the theme of protection by playing one or more humorous commercials from insurance companies. If you don't have access to video in your meeting space, consider using a laptop or tablet—or simply encouraging group members to share their favorite funny commercials on that theme.

> *Note:* Be sure to only play commercials that will be appropriate and inoffensive for the members of your group.

Video Summary: In John 10:7, Jesus says, "I am the door." And in John 10:11, He says, "I am the good shepherd." Jesus is the door by which the sheep go in and out as well as the one who watches over the sheep. For us, this means Jesus is the only means of salvation. And Jesus is the one who protects and watches over us. He establishes boundaries and makes provisions in order for us to have a full and meaningful life.

▶ WATCH THE DVD SEGMENT FOR SESSION 3. THEN USE THE FOLLOWING QUESTIONS AND DISCUSSION POINTS TO TRANSITION INTO THE STUDY.

- Jeff talks about avoiding difficulty versus being delivered from difficulty. As we follow Jesus' direction, we can avoid difficulty and live the full and meaningful life He intends. Share a specific instance when this has this been true for you?
- What about an instance when you had to be delivered from difficulty instead?

WHAT DOES THE BIBLE SAY?

▶ ASK FOR A VOLUNTEER TO READ ALOUD JOHN 10:7-15,27-30.

Response: What's your initial reaction to these verses?

- What questions do you have about these verses?
- What new application do you hope to get from this passage?

▶ TURN THE GROUP'S ATTENTION TO JOHN 10:7-10.

QUESTION 2: Where do we encounter "thieves and robbers" in today's world?

This question requires group members to interpret the biblical text and then encourages them to consider what "thieves and robbers" they encounter in their day-to-day lives. Encourage specific responses.

Optional follow-up: What do you find interesting about Jesus' word pictures in these verses?

▶ MOVE TO JOHN 10:11-13.

QUESTION 3: What do these "I am" statements teach us about Jesus' nature and character?

This question asks group members to interpret the biblical text in terms of what can be learned from this passage about Jesus. Encourage them to look beyond the words.

Optional follow-up: How do we apply these verses to our modern experiences with worship?

Optional activity: Direct group members to complete the activity "The Good Shepherd" on page 27. If time permits, ask volunteers to share what they discovered in the psalm.

▶ CONTINUE WITH JOHN 10:14-15,27-30.

QUESTION 4: What makes Christians question their security in Christ?

If helpful, explain that "security in Christ" refers to people being secure in their salvation. So, what makes some Christians worry about potentially losing their salvation?

Optional follow-up: In what ways have you acted as if your efforts would secure your relationship with God?

QUESTION 5: What's our role in accessing and benefiting from Jesus' protection?

This question calls for application based on the biblical text and is designed to help group members identify their call to action. Encourage them to be specific in their responses. Because this question is broad in scope, be prepared to start the discussion with some ideas of your own.

Optional follow-up: What's our role in helping others do the same?

Note: The following question does not appear in the Bible study book. Use it in your group discussion as time allows.

QUESTION 6: How can we better learn to distinguish Jesus' voice from all others?

This question guides members toward life application. Ask them to keep things practical as they discuss this question. What specific practices have helped them distinguish Jesus' voice from others? As your discussion begins, encourage members to listen closely to the responses of others. Much can be learned in community.

LIVE IT OUT

Encourage group members to consider the following suggestions for how they will respond this week to the offer of Jesus' protection:

- **Identify your fears.** Be especially aware this week of circumstances that cause you to experience fear or concern. Record those moments in a journal or list, and use them as a starting point for prayer.

- **Study Christ.** Read more about the relationship between Jesus and the Father. See page 56 for a short description of what we know about God, and invest time in reading the Scriptures provided.

- **Share what you've learned.** Be intentional about sharing how Jesus has calmed your fears with someone who needs to hear it this week. Pray that God would provide opportunities and conversations that open the door for you to share what you've learned.

Challenge: When fear arises this week, remember your security is in Jesus. Consider spending some time journaling about your fears as they bubble up and how Jesus calms them. These will be good memories to revisit in the future when fear threatens to distract you from the truth.

Pray: Ask for prayer requests and ask group members to pray for the different requests as intercessors. As the leader, close this time by expressing your intention to live without fear in the protection Jesus has offered. Ask for courage and wisdom in sharing the good news of Jesus' ultimate protection with others.

The Point: Jesus is the Resurrection who gives us life now and forever.

The Passage: John 11:17-27

The Setting: Throughout the progression of the Gospel of John, there had been growing opposition to Jesus from the religious establishment. Apart from the overwhelmingly significant teaching that Jesus is the resurrection and the life that comes in John 11, the contextual importance of the chapter comes in the fact that the death of Lazarus, his resuscitation, and the ensuing fallout over the event led the religious authorities to definitively determine Jesus must die (see v. 53).

QUESTION 1: What helps you feel hopeful about the future?

> *Optional activity:* Direct group members to gather into smaller clusters of two to four people. As they talk in these clusters, encourage them to fill in the blank on the following statement with the first thing that comes to mind: "I hope _____." After a couple minutes, direct everyone to re-form new clusters and repeat the experience.

> *Note:* The goal of this exercise is to give people a chance to stand up, move around, share with one another, and introduce the topic of hope.

Video Summary: In John 11:25, Jesus says, "I am the resurrection and the life." Jesus not only has resurrection power, but He is the Resurrection—the Person in whom resurrection resides. We have no power over death and desperately need someone to provide hope when we are in those situations. As believers, we can have confidence that no matter what happens, Jesus is still Lord and able to guarantee life after death.

▶ WATCH THE DVD SEGMENT FOR SESSION 4. THEN USE THE FOLLOWING QUESTIONS AND DISCUSSION POINTS TO TRANSITION INTO THE STUDY.

- When has having confidence in God in the face of death made a difference in your life?
- Who do you need to talk to this week about receiving Jesus so that he or she can experience the same hope we have? Talk with your group about how you can make that happen.

WHAT DOES THE BIBLE SAY?

▶ ASK FOR A VOLUNTEER TO READ ALOUD JOHN 11:17-27.

Response: What's your initial reaction to these verses?

- What do you like about the text?
- What new application do you hope to receive about how to experience a resurrected life?

▶ TURN THE GROUP'S ATTENTION TO JOHN 11:17-24.

QUESTION 2: What do our responses to tragedy reveal about our expectations of God?

This question will give group members an opportunity to share from personal experience. The goal is to help them recognize that their actions and reactions indicate what they truly believe about God and how that may be different from what it is they say they believe about Him.

> ***Optional follow-up:*** What emotions do you experience when you're hoping for something good to happen?

> ***Optional activity:*** Direct group members to complete the activity "The Hope of Heaven" on page 35. If time permits, encourage volunteers to share their responses.

▶ MOVE TO JOHN 11:25-26A.

QUESTION 3: What does this "I am" statement teach us about Jesus' nature and character?

This question asks group members to interpret the biblical text in terms of what can be learned from this passage about Jesus. Encourage them to look beyond the words.

> ***Optional follow-up:*** What part of that is most encouraging to you today? Why?

QUESTION 4: How does Jesus' statement in these verses produce hope?

This question requires that group members interpret the message of the Scripture text to move them toward application. Encourage them to be specific in their responses. To help focus the discussion, consider writing their responses on a white board or tear sheet.

> ***Optional follow-up:*** How would you describe the hope of heaven to someone who's never heard about it?

▶ CONTINUE WITH JOHN 11:26B-27.

QUESTION 5: How does the hope of eternal life influence your daily decisions?

This question offers group members another chance to engage the reality that "eternal life" isn't just something we will experience in the distant future; it's a gift we have already received. Therefore, how does this gift influence our daily decisions?

Note: The following question does not appear in the Bible study book. Use it in your group discussion as time allows.

QUESTION 6: What obstacles prevent us from sharing the hope of eternal and abundant life?

This question will lead group members to examine barriers that sometimes get in the way of sharing the hope they have of eternal and abundant life. Actively participating in this discussion will require them to examine their own experiences and identify stumbling blocks that have been or may still be present. Consider modeling this process by starting the discussion yourself.

Optional follow-up: What obstacles prevent *you* from sharing the hope of eternal and abundant life?

LIVE IT OUT

Jesus is the Resurrection and the life. Invite group members to consider the following options for putting that truth into practice this week:

- **Answer the question.** Take some time to reflect on Jesus' question to Martha regarding His claim to be the Resurrection and the life: "Do you believe this?" Answer that question for your own life.

- **Pray.** Make a list of people within your spheres of influence who have not expressed faith in Jesus. Pray daily for each of those individuals by name.

- **Initiate a conversation.** In addition to praying for those who need to experience Jesus as the resurrection and the life, take the next step of initiating a spiritual conversation with someone on that list. Express what you've experienced in your time as a follower of Christ, and express your desire to see that person know Christ, as well.

Challenge: This can be the year you experience Jesus' resurrection power in a deeper and more meaningful way. Develop a plan and take the steps necessary to know where you stand with Christ—and to help others encounter the One who offers life both now and forever.

Pray: Ask for prayer requests and ask group members to pray for the different requests as intercessors. As the leader, conclude by proclaiming your answer to Jesus' question: "Do you believe this?" Confess your trust in Christ as the only source for resurrection and abundant life both now and forever.

The Point: Jesus is the way to the Father; therefore, we can live in peace.

The Passage: John 14:1-7

The Setting: John began his coverage of Jesus' last week on earth in what we know as chapter 12. By the time he arrived at the passage of this study, it was well into the evening of Jesus' last night on earth. In the upper room only hours before His crucifixion, Jesus devoted Himself to final instructions and assurances the disciples needed before He departed from them.

QUESTION 1: When have you felt most at peace?

> *Optional activity:* As a follow-up to question 1, give your group members two minutes of peace and quiet before continuing the discussion. Encourage everyone to settle into a comfortable spot in your meeting space, and then ask them to relax in whatever mode they choose for a full two minutes. This relaxing could include closing their eyes, playing a game on their phone, chatting with friends, and so on.

> *Note:* Consider adding to the relaxing ambiance of your meeting space by playing soothing music, ocean sounds, or other calming noises in the background.

Video Summary: In John 14:6 Jesus said, "I am the way, the truth, and the life." Jesus is the way—our salvation. Jesus is the truth—the ultimate information about life. Jesus is the life—we can trust Him for eternal life. We will always struggle and know people who are struggling with life challenges. Apart from God, those struggles can cause much anxiety. But if we believe, He can sustain us through any difficulty we face—in life as well as in death.

▶ WATCH THE DVD SEGMENT FOR SESSION 5. THEN USE THE FOLLOWING QUESTIONS AND DISCUSSION POINTS TO TRANSITION INTO THE STUDY.

- What deliberate steps can we take to keep the daily news and world events from so easily overwhelming us?
- Who do you know who is feeling overwhelmed and needs God's message of peace regarding a situation he or she is facing? How will you deliver that message this week?

WHAT DOES THE BIBLE SAY?

▶ ASK FOR A VOLUNTEER TO READ ALOUD JOHN 14:1-7.

Response: What's your initial reaction to these verses?

- What questions do you have about these verses?
- What new application do you hope to get from this passage?

► TURN THE GROUP'S ATTENTION TO JOHN 14:1.

QUESTION 2: How do you determine if someone is trustworthy?

The goal of this question is to set up a parallel between trusting other people and trusting God. By helping group members identify the characteristics that identify other people as trustworthy, they can use those same standards to highlight just how worthy God is of receiving our trust.

> *Optional follow-up:* When do you find it difficult to trust God?

► MOVE TO JOHN 14:2-4.

QUESTION 3: What do you find most comforting in these verses? Why?

Remind group members that there are no "right" answers to this question. People will experience different emotional reactions in terms of how these verses are a comfort to them. Allowing group member to express those emotions creates many benefits.

> *Optional activity:* Direct group members to complete the activity "Personal Assessment: Peace" on page 43.

► CONTINUE WITH JOHN 14:5-7.

QUESTION 4: What does this "I am" statement teach us about Jesus' nature and character?

This question asks group members to interpret the biblical text in terms of what can be learned from this passage about Jesus. Encourage them to look beyond the words.

QUESTION 5: Why is lasting peace found only in Jesus?

It's possible that members of your group may express discomfort (or even disbelief) in the claim that Jesus is the only way to salvation. Don't shut down such thoughts; instead, point to the Scriptures as the source of truth.

> *Optional follow-up:* How would you state the other promises of John 14:1-7 in your own words?

Note: The following question does not appear in the Bible study book. Use it in your group discussion as time allows.

QUESTION 6: Why are so many people tempted to look for peace and purpose outside Christ?

This question will give group members an opportunity to (1) examine, through the filter of this biblical text, how their own personal experiences sometimes cloud the truth; and (2) identify and focus on what they can know is true based on God's Word.

> *Optional follow-up:* What are the implications of Jesus' words for today's culture?

LIVE IT OUT

Jesus is our only Source of true peace during difficulty. Encourage group members to consider the following options for helping others experience this hope this week:

- **Praise God.** Spend an hour thanking Jesus for the place He has prepared for you in heaven. Praise God for blessing you with peace and an eternal home with Christ.

- **Memorize the Word.** Work each day to commit John 14:6 to memory. Encourage friends and family members to join you in memorizing this important verse.

- **Be bold.** Invite a person of a different faith to coffee or lunch. Ask this person to explain what his or her religion teaches about concepts like the way to heaven, truth, and eternal life. In turn, share what Jesus taught and what you believe about these issues.

Challenge: There are times when all of us worry in this world. But we can choose to focus on Christ in even the worst of moments—and in doing so, find the gift of peace. Ask God to make you more aware this week of times when you begin to worry. When you find yourself focusing on the circumstance rather than on Christ, stop immediately and ask Him to restore your peace.

Pray: Ask for prayer requests and ask group members to pray for the different requests as intercessors. As the leader, close this time by praising God for the gift of peace in connection with your eternal salvation. On behalf of yourself and your group, verbally express your commitment to helping others experience the peace of Christ's salvation.

The Point: Jesus is the Vine who empowers us to live productive lives for God.

The Passage: John 15:1-8

The Setting: The setting for this study is similar to that for the previous study with two particular distinctions. It was now somewhat later in the evening, and the location had shifted out of the upper room (see 14:31). Perhaps Jesus and the disciples were making their way to the Mount of Olives and Gethsemane, perhaps they had already arrived, or perhaps they had stopped along the way.

QUESTION 1: When have you felt like a hamster on a wheel?

> ***Optional activity:*** As an object lesson, bring several clusters of grapes to the group gathering. After reading "The Point," pass the grapes around and encourage group members to enjoy a snack taken off the vine.
>
> ***Note:*** If you're in a meeting space where eating wouldn't be appropriate, you could simply display the grapes or a cluster of tomatoes still on the vine as an object lesson.

Video Summary: In John 15:5, Jesus says, "I am the vine; you are the branches." He is the source of all spiritual life and fruit. If we are connected to Jesus, we will produce spiritual fruit. Our lives should be a representation of our connection to Jesus Christ. Spiritual fruit can manifest itself through our lives in a variety of ways. Examples include: leading others to Christ, sacrificial acts of service for God, and character transformation. Glorifying God by producing fruit and giving Him the credit for it is how we prove to be disciples of Christ.

▶ WATCH THE DVD SEGMENT FOR SESSION 6. THEN USE THE FOLLOWING QUESTIONS AND DISCUSSION POINTS TO TRANSITION INTO THE STUDY.

- In what ways have you experienced God's pruning?
- What opportunities is God giving you to exercise your spiritual fruit?

WHAT DOES THE BIBLE SAY?

▶ ASK FOR A VOLUNTEER TO READ ALOUD JOHN 15:1-8.

Response: What's your initial reaction to these verses?

- What questions do you have about what it means to live a productive life for God?
- What new application do you hope to get from this passage?

► TURN THE GROUP'S ATTENTION TO JOHN 15:1-3.

QUESTION 2: What does this "I am" statement teach us about Jesus' nature and character?

This question asks group members to interpret the biblical text in terms of what can be learned from this passage about Jesus. Encourage them to look beyond the words.

> ***Optional follow-up:*** How does pruning make us more productive?

> ***Optional activity:*** Direct group members to complete the activity "Abide in Christ" on page 51. If time permits, encourage volunteers to share their responses.

► MOVE TO JOHN 15:4-7.

QUESTION 3: What does "remaining in Christ" look like in our daily lives?

This question is designed to move group members from Scripture interpretation to life application. Through this process, they will be better able to identify specific experiences in their day-to-day that lead them to remain in Christ.

> ***Optional follow-up:*** What impact does remaining in Christ have on a believer's prayer life?

QUESTION 4: How would you summarize the commands and promises in these verses?

The intent of this question is to prompt interaction with the biblical text. Encourage them to examine the passage closely.

> ***Optional follow-up:*** How does Jesus differentiate between easy love and difficult love in this passage?

► CONTINUE WITH JOHN 15:8.

QUESTION 5: How can we work together to produce fruit?

This is a question that should be engaged and answered by your group as a whole. We often talk about producing fruit as individual disciples of Jesus, but what practical steps can your group take to produce fruit together to the glory of God?

> ***Optional follow-up:*** How does the fruit we produce bring glory to God?

Note: The following question does not appear in the Bible study book. Use it in your group discussion as time allows.

QUESTION 6: What step will you take this week to rely more on Jesus, the Vine, in your daily life?

This question provides group members with an opportunity to identify practical steps for positive actions. Try to steer them away from talking theory; encourage them to get practical.

LIVE IT OUT

Encourage group members to consider the following steps they can take this week to remain in Jesus, the Vine:

- **Double down.** Each day this week, spend twice as much time praying and reading God's Word as you usually do. Take an active step to remain in Christ.

- **Say thanks.** Consider one way God has changed you or used you in recent months. Write a "thank you" letter to God, giving Him glory for the fruit in your life. Consider sharing your letter with those close to you.

- **Plan ahead.** Review your monthly calendar and eliminate any activities that won't bring glory to God. Modify or replace other activities so they can be done in Christ's power and bring glory to Him.

Challenge: We never find ultimate purpose in what we do. Finding purpose is about knowing a Person and allowing Him to shape our lives. Real life—deep, meaningful, satisfying life—comes from connecting to Jesus and allowing His life to flow through ours. Spend some time this week thinking about how you are connecting to Jesus. In what ways are you allowing His life to flow through yours?

Pray: As the leader, close this final session of *More than Enough* in prayer. Thank God for the privilege of studying His Word throughout this resource. Pray that He would grant you the discipline necessary to remain in Christ this week—and that He would reward your efforts with a greater sense of His presence.

Note: If you haven't discussed it yet, decide as a group whether or not you plan to continue to meet together and, if so, what Bible study options you would like to pursue. Visit *LifeWay.com/smallgroups* for help, or if you would like more studies like this one, visit *biblestudiesforlife.com/smallgroups*.

My group's prayer requests

ALSO AVAILABLE ...

SMALL GROUP LEADER KIT

BIBLE STUDIES FOR LIFE

CONNECTED
MY LIFE IN THE CHURCH

THOM S. RAINER

SMALL GROUP MEMBER BOOK

BIBLE STUDIES FOR LIFE

RESILIENT FAITH

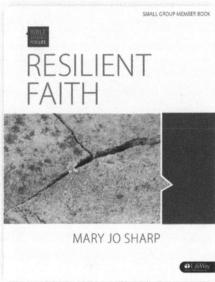

MARY JO SHARP

6-SESSION BIBLE STUDY

BIBLE STUDIES FOR LIFE

STAND STRONG
BUILDING YOUR LIFE ON GOD'S PROMISES

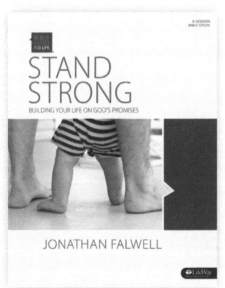

JONATHAN FALWELL

BIBLE STUDIES FOR LIFE

PRESSURE POINTS

CHIP HENDERSON

BIBLE STUDIES FOR LIFE
®

This series helps people understand how to apply the Bible to everyday life—their families, their careers, and their struggles—just as they are, right where they live. A new study releases every three months.

Discover available studies at
biblestudiesforlife.com/smallgroups,
800.458.2772, or at your **LifeWay Christian Store.**

LifeWay
Biblical Solutions for Life